The
Gettysburg Address

by Michael Burgan

Content Adviser: Barbara J. Sanders,
Education Specialist,
Gettysburg National Military Park

Reading Adviser: Rosemary G. Palmer, Ph.D.,
Department of Literacy, College of Education,
Boise State University

COMPASS POINT BOOKS
MINNEAPOLIS, MINNESOTA

Compass Point Books
3109 West 50th Street, #115
Minneapolis, MN 55410

Visit Compass Point Books on the Internet at *www.compasspointbooks.com*
or e-mail your request to *custserv@compasspointbooks.com*

On the cover: Illustration of Abraham Lincoln giving the Gettysburg Address on
November 19, 1863.

Photographs ©: Bettmann/Corbis, cover, 30; Prints Old and Rare, back cover (far left); Library of
Congress, back cover, 18, 20, 24, 27, 40; Stock Montage/Getty Images, 4; MPI/Getty Images, 5,
10, 16, 21, 38; Timothy H. O'Sullivan/MPI/Getty Images, 7, 25; North Wind Picture Archives, 9,
17, 22; National Archives and Records Administration, 11; Kean Collection/Getty Images, 12, 41;
Gettysburg National Military Park, 26; The Granger Collection, New York, 31; Library of
Congress/Getty Images, 34; Herbert Orth/Time Life Pictures/Getty Images, 37.

The version of the Gettysburg Address used on page 33 is the written version recognized by the
Gettysburg National Cemetery, courtesy of the content adviser for this book, Barbara J. Sanders.

Editor: Jacqueline Wolfe
Photo Researcher: Marcie C. Spence
Designer/Page Production: Bradfordesign, Inc./Les Tranby
Cartographer: XNR Productions, Inc.
Educational Consultant: Diane Smolinski

Managing Editor: Catherine Neitge
Creative Director: Keith Griffin
Editorial Director: Carol Jones

Library of Congress Cataloging-in-Publication Data
Burgan, Michael.
    The Gettysburg Address / by Michael Burgan.
    p. cm. — (We the people)
    Includes bibliographical references and index.
    ISBN 0-7565-1271-9 (hard cover)
    1. Lincoln, Abraham, 1809-1865. Gettysburg address—Juvenile literature. 2. United States—
History—Civil War, 1861-1865—Juvenile literature.
I. Title. II. Series: We the people (Series) (Compass Point Books)
    E475.55.B84 2006
    973.7'349—dc22   2005002473

TABLE OF CONTENTS

BURYING THE DEAD

For three days in July 1863, one of the bloodiest battles of the Civil War raged in and around the town of Gettysburg, Pennsylvania. Confederate troops led by

General Robert E. Lee sought their first major victory in the North. Lee hoped that if he won, the Union might want to end the war. Lee also hoped to draw Union troops away from Virginia, where Richmond—the capital of the Confederate states— was located.

Robert E. Lee on his horse, Traveller, directed the Battle of Gettysburg.

4

In Pennsylvania, Lee knew that when supplies ran low, his men could get what they needed from the people of Gettysburg. In fact, a Confederate brigade had been going to get supplies when they ran into some Union cavalry scouts. The two sides literally stumbled onto one another just outside Gettysburg.

More than 165,000 soldiers fought during the Battle of Gettysburg.

During those three days in July 1863, more than 165,000 soldiers from the Union and Confederate armies marched through the fields and woods of Gettysburg. They fought on rolling hills and among orchards. Cannons boomed and guns fired, creating clouds of smoke that clung to the battlefield. Men screamed and cried as bullets cut them down. Hearing the sounds of war, one newspaper reporter wrote, "The valley … seemed alive with demons." Of the men who fought, approximately 51,000 of them became casualties.

In the end, Lee's bold plan failed. The Union army defeated the Confederate army at Gettysburg. Even though the Civil War dragged on for almost two more years, Gettysburg was a significant battle. The Confederacy lost any chance of gaining aid from foreign countries. These nations did not want to support a losing side. And the Union was determined to fight until the North and South were once again one country—the United States of America.

When the Battle of Gettysburg ended, thousands of dead soldiers from both sides lay on the battlefield. Many were barely covered with dirt. Local and state officials decided that the Union troops needed proper burials. By the fall, many of the dead were resting in Gettysburg's new Soldiers' National Cemetery. Confederate soldiers, on the other hand, were buried in trench graves where they fell.

Dead bodies littered the fields and forests around Gettysburg.

On November 19, 1863, President Abraham Lincoln went to the dedication of the Gettysburg cemetery. He spoke for less than three minutes—his speech was just 269 words long. But in those few words, Lincoln explained the meaning of the Civil War. The country had to be united, and it had to work for equality. The goal was to make sure that "government of the people, by the people, and for the people, shall not perish from the earth."

Lincoln said that he doubted future Americans would remember what was said that day in Gettysburg. The great president was wrong. His Gettysburg Address is one of the most famous speeches in history. People still read it today because Lincoln so clearly stated the goals of the United States. Lincoln said the United States was founded as a democracy to protect the equal rights of all citizens.

SLAVERY IN AMERICA

Abraham Lincoln was elected president in 1860, when Americans were arguing over slavery. Most white Southerners favored slavery, while most Northerners opposed it. Southern plantation owners relied on African-American slaves to raise their crops and act as servants in their homes. The Southern economy was deeply tied to slavery.

Even though most Union states had outlawed slavery, free blacks in the North still faced limits on what they could do. They often experienced discrimination in housing, education, and legal rights. Starting in the 1840s, a growing

The Southern economy was tied to slavery because of the need for field labor.

9

A group of abolitionists, known as the Oberlin Rescuers, after they rescued a fugitive slave from a jail in Ohio

number of Northerners began to oppose slavery and the unequal treatment of free blacks. They believed African-Americans deserved the same freedom and rights as whites. People who worked to abolish, or end, slavery in the United States were called abolitionists.

Many abolitionists opposed slavery for religious reasons, claiming God made everyone equal. Some abolitionists also looked for support in the Declaration of Independence of 1776. With that document, American political leaders rejected British control over the 13 American colonies. The colonies established a new, independent nation called the United States. One of the most famous lines of the declaration states that "all men are created equal." Abolitionists believed this applied to African-Americans as well.

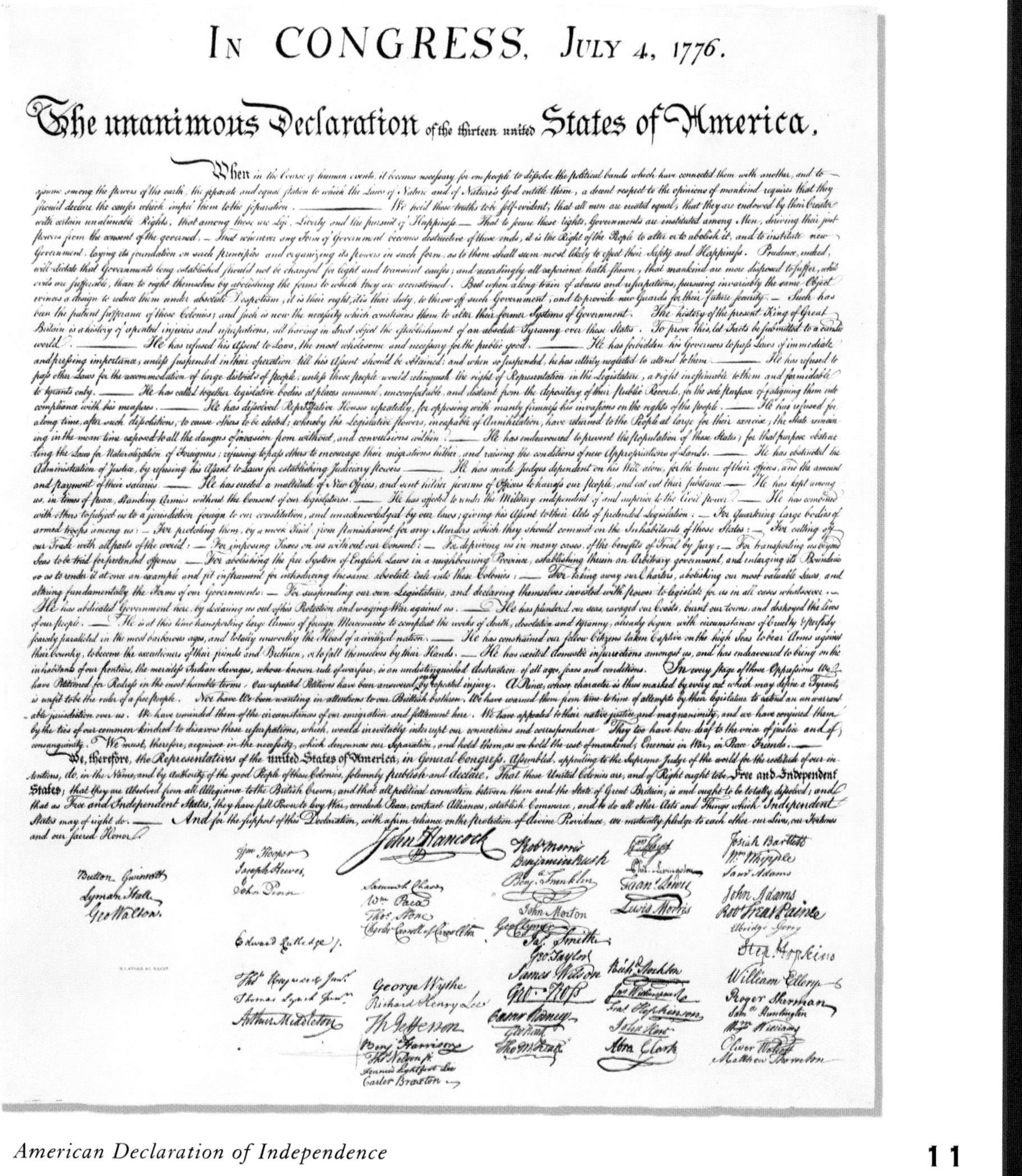

American Declaration of Independence

LINCOLN AND SLAVERY

In 1846, Abraham Lincoln was elected to represent Illinois in the U.S. House of Representatives. This branch of the government, along with the Senate, makes laws. At the time, slavery was a key issue. Slave owners said new states created in the West should be allowed to have slavery if their residents so chose. Other Americans did not want slavery in new states, yet

Lincoln and other politicians heavily debated the issue of slavery.

they did not want to abolish slavery everywhere. Only abolitionists wanted an immediate, complete end to slavery, but they lacked the power to make it happen.

Lincoln was opposed to slavery and said he hoped it would eventually die a natural death. Illinois was a free state where slavery was not allowed. Yet in 1848, voters made it illegal for free blacks to move to Illinois. In addition, some Illinois residents supported slavery. Now, if Lincoln spoke supporting the total abolishment of slavery, he would anger many voters. In some speeches, he suggested that whites were superior to blacks. Yet Lincoln thought slavery was evil. And in a speech he made in 1858, he pointed out that the Declaration of Independence states that African-Americans were equal to whites. Blacks and whites both had the "right to life, liberty, and the pursuit of happiness … This they [the authors of the Declaration] said, and this they meant."

When Lincoln ran for president in 1860, he promised the South he would not abolish slavery there. He said each state should decide whether to accept it or not. White

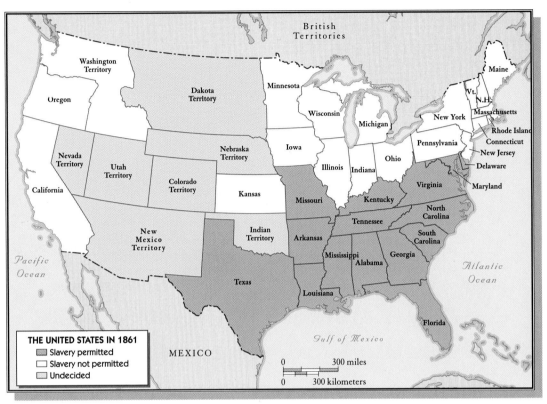

The issue of slavery split the nation in half.

Southerners, however, did not trust Lincoln. After his election, some Southern states began to secede, or break away, from the Union because they feared Lincoln would try to end slavery across the United States. They believed the only way to protect slavery was to form their own country. They called this new nation the Confederate States of America. It was often called the Confederacy.

14

THE CIVIL WAR BEGINS

Lincoln was inaugurated as the U.S. president on March 4, 1861. By then, the Confederate states had already written a constitution. This document outlined what kind of government the South would have. In his first public speech as president, Lincoln argued that the South could not legally secede. He said, "No state upon its own mere motion can lawfully get out of the Union." Lincoln saw the Confederates as rebels. He believed the U.S. Constitution gave him the right to end any rebellion in order to keep the Union whole.

In April 1861, Confederate forces attacked Fort Sumter, a Union fort in South Carolina. The Confederate troops quickly took control of the Union fort. Lincoln soon called for 75,000 volunteers to join the Union Army. He wanted to fight to bring the Confederate states back into the Union. The Civil War had begun.

Fort Sumter was an important victory for the Confederates.

The Union seemed to have a better chance of winning the war. The North had more white men of military age. The North also owned more factories that produced weapons and supplies. When the Civil War began, both sides thought it would end quickly. Southerners believed that the North would field an army of weaklings with no real appetite for fighting.

16

Factory workers making rifle cartridges

Northerners, meanwhile, viewed Southern soldiers
as disorganized and thought the undisciplined troops
would be easily overwhelmed by superior Union
firepower. A Chicago newspaper even boasted that
"Illinois can whip the South by herself." But white
Southerners were defending their beloved land, homes,
families, and way of life.

Because of its skilled commanders and some Union blunders, the Confederacy won the first major battle, Bull Run in Virginia. But the next major battle

Many abolitionists, including Passmore Williamson, secretary of the Pennsylvania Abolition Society, spent time in jail because of their anti-slavery efforts.

at Shiloh, Tennessee, was a Union victory. The Confederacy's main goal was to defend its own land, not invade and capture Union territory. The Union army had the much harder job of invading the South and forcing it to surrender. Over time, however, the Union Army had many military successes. These victories prompted abolitionists to speak out even more aggressively. They wanted the Civil War to lead to the emancipation, or freeing, of slaves.

At first, Lincoln resisted the abolitionists. He stated over and over again that the main purpose of the war was to save the Union, not to end slavery. The Union included four states that allowed slavery: Missouri, Kentucky, Delaware, and Maryland. Lincoln feared these states might join the Confederacy if he freed their slaves.

By September 1862, Lincoln saw a way to please the abolitionists and not upset the slave states in the Union. He issued a statement called the Emancipation Proclamation.

Abraham Lincoln and his Emancipation Proclamation

As of January 1, 1863, all slaves located in the rebellious Southern states were considered free. The Emancipation Proclamation, however, did not free slaves in the four border states that allowed slavery, but had remained loyal to the Union. Lincoln hoped slaves would run away from their masters and help the Union fight the South. The Emancipation Proclamation also let free blacks in the North join the Union Army. These volunteers would provide fresh troops at a time when many whites in the North did not want to join the Army.

Joining the Union Army empowered African-Americans to fight for the freedom of other African-Americans.

Lincoln said he issued the Emancipation Proclamation as part of his duties as commander in chief. In that role, a U.S. president directs the military. Lincoln still did not say emancipation was a moral issue. Instead he said that freeing the slaves was a good

Abraham Lincoln

military move. But the proclamation meant that the Civil War was not just about keeping the Union whole. Lincoln was clearly stating the Union's goal to end slavery in the South.

22

Six months passed between the Emancipation Proclamation going into effect in January and the Battle of Gettysburg. During that time, some Northerners wanted Lincoln to say more about the goals of the war. A few people told Lincoln that all Americans needed to hear why winning the war was so important. Others wanted Lincoln to talk about what would happen after the war if the North won. The U.S. government would need to find a way to bring the Confederacy back into the Union. The rights of several million newly freed blacks would also be a concern. Also, the sight of Union blood being shed on Northern soil upset the Northerners greatly. Lincoln knew discussing these concerns was important. He would have a chance to speak publicly about some of them soon enough.

GETTYSBURG AND ITS CEMETERY

After the Union victory at Gettysburg, corpses littered the land. Union General George Meade kept his troops moving, saying, "I cannot delay to pick up the debris of the battlefield." In the summer heat, the sickening smell of rotting corpses filled the air. Some dead soldiers were buried, but not very deep. A local lawyer named David Wills wrote a letter to Pennsylvania's governor describing the scene in Gettysburg:

Major General George G. Meade (front) and his staff

"My attention has been directed to several places where the hogs were actually rooting out the bodies and devouring them."

Wills was appointed by the governor to do something about the dead bodies. He originally planned on identifying the bodies of Union soldiers and sending them to their families, but because of the difficulty of identification and the risk of contracting illnesses, that plan was quickly dismissed. By the end of July, the idea for a national cemetery had been suggested, and the 18 Union states quickly agreed.

The National Soldiers' Cemetery was created next to the local cemetery.

Workers began to roam through Gettysburg, looking for Union corpses. They searched for something on the bodies that revealed who the soldiers were and which state they came from. Some soldiers had wooden tags or metal

Homemade metal tag from the Civil War

discs with their names printed on them. However, 685 dead Union soldiers at Gettysburg were only identifiable by the state they were from and 979 lacked anything that showed who they were. They were later buried in graves marked "unknown." Confederate bodies were put into trenches, with approximately 100 bodies per trench.

Wills wanted a public ceremony to dedicate the new cemetery. He asked Edward Everett of Massachusetts to give the main speech. Everett, a minister and teacher, had also been a vice presidential candidate, the secretary of state, and the president of Harvard College. He was famous for his long, sentimental, and thoughtful speeches. When President Lincoln heard about the ceremony, he said he would attend. When Wills heard that, he had to think of some way to get the president involved.

Edward Everett

27

Wills formally invited Lincoln on November 2. He asked the president to "formally set apart these grounds to their sacred use." Lincoln knew he would not be the main speaker at the ceremony, but he knew he could use the event to explain to the country what he felt was the Union's purpose in the war.

WRITING AND GIVING THE ADDRESS

The ceremony at Gettysburg cemetery was scheduled for November 19. Many stories have been told about how Lincoln wrote his address. Some people claimed he quickly scribbled it down just before he gave it. Most historians don't believe this because Lincoln was known to take his time before writing any important speech or paper. He probably began writing the speech in Washington, D.C., after thinking about what he would say. On November 18, he took the train to Gettysburg. He may have worked on the speech along the way. He made his last changes while staying at David Wills' house the night before the ceremony.

The morning of November 19 was sunny, after nighttime rains. As many as 20,000 people streamed into Soldiers' National Cemetery for the dedication. Lincoln spent part of the morning walking through the

Gettysburg battlefield. Then he went back to Wills' house to dress for his speech. As usual, he wore a black suit.

Lincoln, thought to be the man in the top hat and long black coat, arrived at Gettysburg by train.

Lincoln rode a horse to the cemetery, and people lined the parade route to see him and the others. At the cemetery, Birgfield's Band of Philadelphia played

Thousands attended the dedication of the Soldiers' National Cemetery.

and a minister said a prayer. Messages sent from illustrious people who had been unable to attend were read, and at noon Edward Everett began to speak.

Everett had carefully studied what happened during the Battle of Gettysburg. He gave a detailed account of the battle. Everett clearly blamed the South for starting the Civil War and killing the thousands of Union soldiers buried in the cemetery. He referred to the "disloyal slaveholders of the South" and called for "the complete destruction of the military power of the enemy." Everett spoke for almost two hours.

The Baltimore Glee Club sang a hymn, and then President Lincoln was introduced. At the beginning of the speech, Lincoln's voice was described as "shrill, almost squeaky," but after he got underway, his voice "lost its piping quality, turning melodious, almost musical" as he delivered these words:

"Four score and seven years ago our fathers brought forth on this continent, a new nation, conceived in Liberty, and dedicated to the proposition that all men are created equal.

Now we are engaged in a great civil war, testing whether that nation, or any nation so conceived and so dedicated, can long endure. We are met on a great battle-field of that war. We have come to dedicate a portion of that field, as a final resting place for those who here gave their lives that that nation might live. It is altogether fitting and proper that we should do this.

But, in a larger sense, we cannot dedicate—we cannot consecrate—we can not hallow—this ground. The brave men, living and dead, who struggled here, have consecrated it, far above our poor power to add or detract. The world will little note, nor long remember what we say here, but it can never forget what they did here. It is for us the living, rather, to be dedicated here to the unfinished work which they who fought here have thus far so nobly advanced. It is rather for us to be here dedicated to the great task remaining before us—that from these honored dead we take increased devotion to that cause for which they gave the last full measure of devotion—that we here highly resolve that these dead shall not have died in vain—that this nation, under God, shall have a new birth of freedom—and that government of the people, by the people, for the people, shall not perish from the earth."

33

It is reported there was "perfect silence" as Lincoln spoke at Gettysburg.

Lincoln used an unusual phrase to open his speech. "Four score and seven" is the same as eighty-seven. Lincoln was referring to biblical language, that sometimes used the word "score" to represent 20 years. He knew most Americans read the Bible and would understand what he meant. It is supposed that Lincoln was trying to suggest that God played a role in American life. Other words he chose also referred to religion. The men who created the United States were "fathers," Lincoln said, and God was also sometimes called a father. To consecrate something is to make it holy and sacred.

In noting the years, Lincoln was talking about something special that happened 87 years earlier. In 1776, the American colonies declared their independence from Great Britain. To Lincoln, the key idea of the Declaration of Independence was that all Americans were equal. If they were equal under the law, then no one could be held in slavery. Without mentioning slavery, Lincoln suggested that the Civil War was being fought to end it.

The war was also about keeping the United States a free and democratic country. The Declaration of Independence said that a government's powers come from the people who formed the country. Through the Constitution, the American people had decided what powers their government should have. Lincoln saw the declaration as the first political statement of American citizens. Its call for equality was still the country's main goal—even though equality was not mentioned in the Constitution.

Like Everett, Lincoln praised the soldiers who fought and died at Gettysburg. But unlike Everett, he did not talk about the Confederates as the Union's enemy. He did not blame them for the bodies buried at the cemetery. He believed the North and South were still united, even though they were at war. He reminded the Union that its goal was to win the war and keep a democratic government in the United States.

The Gettysburg Address showed Lincoln's talents as a writer and thinker. He talked very directly, establishing the Declaration of Independence as the guiding conscience of the country and challenging the country to live up to its ideals. He did all this with very few words and without naming the enemy soldiers or government.

Executive Mansion,

Washington, _____ , 186 .

Four score and seven years ago our fathers brought forth, upon this continent, a new nation, conceived in liberty, and dedicated to the proposition that "all men are created equal"

Now we are engaged in a great civil war, testing whether that nation, or any nation so conceived, and so dedicated, can long endure. We are met on a great battle field of that war. We have come to dedicate a portion of it, as a final resting place for those who died here, that the nation might live. This we may, in all propriety do. But, in a larger sense, we can not dedicate— we can not consecrate— we can not hallow, this ground— The brave men, living and dead, who struggled here, have hallowed it, far above our poor power to add or detract. The world will little note, nor long remember what we say here; while it can never forget what they did here.

It is rather for us, the living, to stand here,

Handwritten draft of President Abraham Lincoln's Gettysburg Address

AFTER THE SPEECH

By one report, Lincoln was not sure his speech had gone well. There had been perfect silence during the entire speech. "Not a word, not a cheer, not a shout," was heard, reported a newspaperman near the front. A long burst of applause came after Lincoln finished. Edward Everett later praised the speech. Lincoln wrote to him, "I am pleased to know that … the little I did say was not entirely a failure." Several newspapers also praised the address. One Illinois paper wrote that Lincoln's words had "verbal perfection and beauty."

Lincoln standing near a copy of the Gettysburg Address

Other Northerners, however, attacked Lincoln. They did not think he should have implied that Union soldiers had died to end slavery. One Chicago newspaper noted that the Constitution allowed slavery and said the goal of the war should be merely to keep the Union whole. Lincoln, however, had already decided the Civil War should end slavery once and for all.

With his address over, Lincoln stayed in Gettysburg for a little while to meet some local people and then returned to Washington. He had started feeling ill while in Gettysburg, and he spent the next two weeks in bed with a mild case of smallpox. Still, as president, he had plenty of work to do. The war was still going on. Union and Confederate troops fought in Tennessee, Georgia, and Virginia. Lincoln was also thinking about the presidential election of 1864. He was a Republican, and members of his own party did not agree on key issues. Some wanted Lincoln to harshly punish Confederate leaders when the war ended. Others believed Lincoln should go easy on the

Lincoln taking the oath at his second inauguration on March 4, 1865.

South. Lincoln also had to deal with Democrats, many of whom were against the war from the beginning. They wanted Lincoln out of office and the fighting to end as soon as possible.

Lincoln won the election of November 1864. By this time, it was clear that the North would win the war. In March 1865, he gave his second inaugural speech. Unlike the Gettysburg Address, Lincoln talked openly about slavery. He said all Americans knew that slavery "was, somehow, the cause of the war." He felt the Civil War was God's way of bringing slavery to an end in the United States. He closed by saying he hoped all Americans would work together to heal the destruction and pain caused by the war.

John Wilkes Booth shot President Abraham Lincoln in the president's box at Ford's Theater, April 14, 1865.

President Lincoln never had a chance to help with that healing. On April 9, Confederate General Robert E. Lee surrendered to Union General Ulysses S. Grant. Less than one week later, Abraham Lincoln was dead. John Wilkes Booth, a supporter of the Confederacy, shot the president in the back of the head while he attended a play.

Abraham Lincoln made many speeches in his political career. His writings fill several large books. Yet his short speech at Gettysburg remains quite possibly the most powerful words of his life. According to historian Garry Wills, Lincoln made the idea of equality a major goal of the U.S. government. "Because of it," Wills wrote, "we live in a different America."

GLOSSARY

casualties—soldiers killed, wounded, captured, or reported missing after a battle

Confederacy—the Southern states that fought against the Northern states in the Civil War; also called the Confederate States of America

constitution—a document stating the basic rules of a government

corpses—dead bodies

dedicate—to officially open a public space; to set aside a space for a special use

democracy—a form of government in which the people elect their leaders

discrimination—treating people unfairly because of their race, religion, sex, or age

inauguration—a president's swearing-in ceremony

sacred—holy or worthy of deep respect

Union—the United States of America; also the Northern states that fought against the Southern states in the Civil War

DID YOU KNOW?

- Several versions of the Gettysburg Address exist. Reporters who heard Lincoln give his speech noted some words that were not in the original written speech. Several different written versions also exist. The version used in this book is the written version recognized by the Gettysburg National Cemetery.

- Just over 3,500 Union soldiers are buried at the Soldiers' National Cemetery. U.S. soldiers who died in later wars are also buried there.

- Edward Everett did not look at his written speeches when he spoke. He recited even the longest addresses from memory.

- About 10,000 horses died at the Battle of Gettysburg. Their bodies were burned.

- Abraham Lincoln personally wrote out five copies of the Gettysburg Address. The first two are at the Library of Congress, the third is at Illinois's State Historical Library, the fourth is at Cornell University in New York, and the last one he wrote is in Washington, D.C., in the Lincoln Room in the White House.

IMPORTANT DATES

Timeline

1809	Abraham Lincoln is born near Hodgenville, Kentucky, on February 12.
1846	Lincoln is elected to the U.S. House of Representatives.
1860	Lincoln is elected U.S. president in November; the first of 11 Southern states leaves the Union to form the Confederate States of America in December.
1861	Civil War begins in April.
1863	Lincoln frees Southern slaves with the Emancipation Proclamation in January; Union and Confederate forces battle in Gettysburg, Pennsylvania in July; Lincoln delivers the Gettysburg Address in November.
1864	Lincoln is elected president for a second time in November.
1865	The main Southern army surrenders on April 9; John Wilkes Booth shoots President Lincoln on April 14; Lincoln dies on April 15.

IMPORTANT PEOPLE

JOHN WILKES BOOTH (1838–1865)
Supporter of the Confederacy who killed Abraham Lincoln

EDWARD EVERETT (1794–1865)
Main speaker at the dedication of the Gettysburg cemetery

ULYSSES S. GRANT (1822–1885)
General who accepted Robert E. Lee's surrender at the end of the Civil War; he later was elected president and served two terms

ROBERT E. LEE (1807–1870)
General who led Southern troops at the Battle of Gettysburg

ABRAHAM LINCOLN (1809–1865)
President of the United States during the Civil War

GEORGE G. MEADE (1815–1872)
General who led Northern troops at the Battle of Gettysburg

DAVID WILLS (1831–1894)
Lawyer who organized the Soldiers' National Cemetery in Gettysburg, Pennsylvania

WANT TO KNOW MORE?

At the Library

Feinberg, Barbara Silberdick. *Abraham Lincoln's Gettysburg Address: Four Score and More.* Brookfield, Conn.: Twenty-First Century Books, 2000.

McPherson, James. *Fields of Fury: The American Civil War.* New York: Atheneum Books for Young Readers, 2002.

Slavicek, Louise Shipley. *Abraham Lincoln.* Philadelphia: Chelsea House Publishers, 2004.

Tanaka, Shelley. *Gettysburg: The Legendary Battle and the Address That Inspired a Nation.* New York: Hyperion Books for Children, 2003.

On the Web

For more information on the *Gettysburg Address,* use FactHound to track down Web sites related to this book.

1. Go to *www.facthound.com*

2. Type in a search word related to this book or this book ID: 0756512719

3. Click on the *Fetch It* button.

Your trusty FactHound will fetch the best Web sites for you!

On the Road

Gettysburg National Military Park

97 Taneytown Road

Gettysburg, PA 17325-2804

717/334-1124

To visit both the Gettysburg
battlefield and cemetery

**Abraham Lincoln Presidential
Library and Museum**

1 Old State Capitol Plaza

Springfield, Illinois 62701

217/524-7216

To learn more about Abraham
Lincoln's presidency and view
exhibits on his life

Look for more We the People books about this era:

*The Assassination of
    Abraham Lincoln*

The Battle of Gettysburg

The Carpetbaggers

The Emancipation Proclamation

Great Women of the Civil War

The Underground Railroad

A complete list of We the People titles is available on our Web site:
www.compasspointbooks.com

INDEX

About the Author

Michael Burgan is a freelance writer of books for children and adults. A history graduate of the University of Connecticut, he has written more than 90 fiction and nonfiction children's books for various publishers. For adult audiences, he has written news articles, essays, and plays. Michael Burgan is a recipient of an Educational Press Association of America award.